PETER ETHERIDGE.

AN ALBUM OF
OLD HORSHAM

TONY WALES

Ensign
PUBLICATIONS

Published by Ensign Publications
2 Redcar Street, Shirley, Southampton SO1 5LL

ISBN 185455 011 X

Designed by Mark Eslick

Typeset by R.A. Design, New Milton, Hants

Jacket front: **EAST STREET, c1903.** Looking towards Middle Street.

Jacket back: **HORSHAM GOODS YARD, c1905.** Locomotive shed.

ACKNOWLEDGEMENTS

The author would like to acknowledge in particular my valued friend Cecil Cramp for his unfailing help and advice with this and my other books. Among others who gave invaluable help are the Misses Boxall, Mr G. Coomber, Mr and Mrs G. Etheridge, Mr R. Glaysher, Mrs Howard, Mrs McGrath, Mr T. Mills, Mr J. Payne, Mrs P. Tidey, Mr M. Veness, Mr I. Wale, Mrs C. Wales.

Other books by Tony Wales

We Wunt be Druv (1976)
A Sussex Garland (1979)
The West Sussex Village Book (1984)
Horsham in Old Picture Postcards (1987)

INTRODUCTION

Throughout a long and varied history, Horsham has seen many changes. Once important as an assize town, and a thriving centre for the sale of agricultural produce from the surrounding countryside, it has developed in modern times into one of the largest towns in North Sussex. The population, now approximately 30,000, has risen rapidly in recent years, and seems set to continue to grow. The factors contributing most to its continued expansion, are it's accessibility to London and to the enlarged Gatwick Airport to the north, and the excellent communications offered by the M23 and M25 motorways. Other changes in recent years have been the loss of many small family businesses, which once dominated the main shopping streets of the town and the gain of many light industries located on several industrial estates, which now replace the farms and brickfields which once occupied several locations within the town itself. Earlier still, Horsham was noted for its iron works which were carried on within the wooded areas to the North-east. Now all that remains of these are several large stretches of water known as Hammer ponds — beloved of local fishermen and nature lovers.

Several roads have been renamed at different times — Butcher's Row, where meat from bull-baiting carried on in the Carfax was once sold, has become the more prosaic Middle Street. Back Lane is now Park Street, the Bishopric is no longer popularly known as "The Rookery". Other roads have disappeared entirely, such as Albion Road and Albion Terrace, and there are of course many new roads — some in the centre of the town (Albion Way, Swan Walk and Black Horse Way) and many more in the new housing estates on the fringes. The new Northern Bypass will be completed by 1989, and there will be much new development between the present built-up area and the edges of the bypass. On the Northern side of Horsham, a large nature reserve, including the attractive Warnham mill pond, has just been opened on land acquired by the Council from the Lucas Family.

At the present time changes in the town centre are beginning which will be the most momentous to take place at any single time in Horsham's history. The face of Horsham will be changed in many different ways, and the whole character of what was once a quiet country town will be completely transformed. Minor landmarks, which older residents once took for granted, are disappearing overnight, and those who have lived in Horsham all their lives wonder how much longer they will be able to find anything recognisable.

Thankfully one of Horsham's oldest and loveliest streets remains relatively unscathed — the Causeway which leads from Market Square to the beautiful Parish Church of St. Mary the Virgin. The trees have been replaced, and the road surface which once had stepping stones across the puddles, has been properly surfaced; but most of the old houses remain, an air of peace and tranquility continues. This and Horsham Park, in the middle of the town, are two of Horsham's remaining jewels, and such they will surely remain. These apart, all around is change, and even residents who came to the town as recently as twenty years ago, are expressing surprise at the scale and pace of the alterations during such a brief period. Many older residents still

refer to parts of the town by their original names, once associated with a building which stood near-by (The Black Horse Corner, for instance, although Black Horse Hotel has long disappeared), much to the mystification of newer residents. Perhaps sometimes they do it intentionally, just as my mother always insisted on calling a well known grocers, Evershed and Cripps, by its much earlier name of Churchmans.

With all these changes, whether for better or worse, it does seen a very suitable time to bring out this book, showing how Horsham has altered and grown during the life of the camera. Some of the pictures go back to the earliest possible date for a photo, and some even a little before the first photographic image. At the same time I have included a few of more modern times, where they show scenes which no longer exist.

The main shopping streets in the town were traditionally West, Middle and East. Although we have a South Street, it is so short as to be almost non-existent. West Street is now a pedestrian precinct, and has relinquished its role as Horsham's "High Street" to Swan Walk and Swan Square, which are now to be extended and enclosed.

Middle Street, no longer the daily scene of carters arguing as they tried to pass each other with their carts, is now also paved, and East Street may be similarly treated.

The historic Carfax is still the centre of the town, and may also be transformed into a paved area. For as long as many can remember it has been the starting and stopping place for the many bus services which ran into, or from Horsham. Now the buses are smaller and less, and eventually may disappear from the Carfax altogether. Once it was the home of the fairs and bonfires, until the nuisance these caused to residents brought their removal to a less built-up area to the west of the town. Now many would like to see the Saturday Market, at present located in an enclosed piece of ground on the edge of the Carfax, moved into the Carfax itself, to become a lively, focal point.

The Town hall (sometimes now spoken of as "The Old Town Hall") once housed the Council Chamber and the Court Room. It is an interesting looking building, appearing deceptively old, although actually only built in its present form in 1888 (it included some parts of an earlier building). It is viewed with a mixture of affection and exasperation by the motorists who have difficulty in negotiating the narrow stretch of roadway on the west side. There is now a new Council Chamber in the District Council's recently built Park North, in North Street. There is also a relatively new Court House in Hurst Road, connected to the police station which lies to the rear of it, by an underground passage. Before this was built, the police headquarters were in Barttelot Road, and included a red lamp outside the main entrance, rather than the more customary blue one.

Of our older buildings, the Parish Church is perhaps the most important. It is a blend of Norman, 13th, 14th and 15th century work, and is considered one of the finest parish churches in the weald of Sussex. Restorations costing over £8,000 were carried out in 1864-5. Not a large figure by present values, but a lot of money at the time. The spire is handsome, although it has a definite lean to the south. It is covered by 50,000 wooden shingles, the belfry houses bells dating from 1752. The flagstones around the church and much of the paving in the Causeway are of the famous Horsham stone, which was once quarried to the south-west of Horsham. Park House, which was built in the 17th century and enlarged in the 18th, was originally the home of the Hurst family, the name surviving in Hurst Road, Avenue and Court, and in other ways.

Many of Horsham's oldest and most interesting houses are in the Causeway, including Causeway House, which serves as a fitting home for Horsham Museum. The house is at least as old as 15th century, although an earlier building is believed to have existed on the site. The Museum was founded in 1893 by members of the Horsham Free Christian Church in Worthing Road. In 1929 it was moved to Horsham Park House, remaining there until 1941 when the collection was moved to its present home. It is particularly rich in local history and has a permanent, professional staff. Also in the Causeway is Manor House, once a private dwelling, then a school, and now the national headquarters of the Royal Society for the Prevention of Cruelty to Animals. The Barn, originally within the Manor House grounds, is now owned by the Parish Church and is used for a variety of functions, and houses a small chapel.

An interesting street is the Bishopric, once the home of Horsham's cattle market, and also the birthplace of probably Horsham's most famous "character", old Henry Burstow who wrote his recollections of the town in 1911, leaving us a book which has been the greatest source of 19th century social history for local writers ever since.

On the north-east of the town there is St. Leonard's Forest, once said to be the haunt of smugglers, and strange spirits including a headless horseman, a dragon and Mick

Miles (or Mike Mills) who ran a race with the Devil.

There were several wind and water mills in and around Horsham, and like most towns and villages up to the last century, it was largely self-supporting, with many small businesses covering every possible local need. Smuggling was rife, with much illicit material travelling through Horsham on its way from the coast to London. It was also a military town, remembered by such names as Barrack Fields and Depot Road.

I hope that older residents will have their memories pleasantly jolted by this book, and that newer Horshamites will also enjoy seeing something of Horsham as it was.

CONTENTS

An early view of Horsham's main shopping street, West Street, probably about 1885. The most notable shop is Albery, the saddle and harness maker. The shop no longer exists, although much of its contents are in Horsham Museum. Looking west towards the Bishopric the next shop is Price and Co, printers, another old Horsham business. The street lamps, affixed to shops, are few and far between.

The early shop front of Jury Cramp, watchmakers and jewellers, at No 3 and 4 West Street (No 4 had previously been Horsham's Post Office). The business which began in Market Square in 1872, moved to Middle Street, and then to West Street in 1878, which was when this photograph was taken.

A general view of West Street from the west end, very early in this century. The imposing Black Horse Hotel and the neighbouring Corn Exchange are on the right of the picture. Later the Corn Exchange building was incorporated into the Black Horse Hotel, which also lent its name to this busy corner. Now the name exists only in the service road behind the West Street shops, which is known as Black Horse Way.

8

Another general view of West Street c.1908, again from the West end, but moving along towards Middle Street. One of Horsham's attractive lamp standards can be seen, as well as the infamous clock which always stood at five to nine, and just above it the figure of an eagle, said to have been originally a trade mark of a brewery. The gentleman with his dog crossing the street is Mr William Albery, noted local historian.

Farley's at No. 50 West Street, about 1908, reputed to be Horsham's oldest shop front. They sold corn, seed, hay, cake, poultry and game foods, manures and garden seeds. One of the incidental attractions of the shop was the delightful mixture of smells. On the right can be seen the corner of The Swan Hotel, one of West Street's well-known hostelries.

The Home & Colonial Stores at No. 58 West Street about 1928. This was the heyday of the small, multiple grocers, which were replacing some of the local firms. West Street had The International Stores, Walker's Stores, Liptons, The Maypole and David Gregg. This is a typical West Street grocer's window from this period, and includes the memorable sales pitch "Spending means Saving at the H&C."

Hunt Brothers (Silk mercers & general drapers) soon after their arrival in Horsham. The windows are small and apart from a showcase do not extend around the corner into South Street. The roof of Horsham stone with its characteristic undulating surface, can be clearly seen.

Another view of Hunt Brothers on the West Street and South Street corner, about 1885. The premises are now somewhat grander than in the last picture, and a number of items of stock have strayed outside. Hunts had the honour of being number one and two West Street, something which I am sure they appreciated, as they were always very proud of the prestige of their business.

The date is now about 1890 and Hunt Brothers have rebuilt their corner site completely, incorporating this imposing cupola topped with a flag-pole. The new shop windows are lit by their own lamps, something which was common for many shops of this period. The items of clothing hanging outside have disappeared, a good deal of trouble seems to have been taken over the window displays.

14

WEST STREET, HORSHAM.

A final picture of the West Street-South Street corner site. We are now well into the present century, the Capital and Counties Bank has replaced Hunts, although the latter were still trading at No. 2 next to the bank. The corner still boasts a bank — Lloyds, shortly to be re-furbished but of course the facade will be retained.

Seagrave the Bakers on the corner of Bishopric and Springfield Road around 1935. The aroma from local baker's shops was a tremendous lure for all the children in the neighbourhood. Just as the corner opposite was known as Black Horse Corner, so this was known as Piggott's Corner. This was the corner which boasted Horsham's first traffic lights. Some of the locals would congregate here on summer evenings to watch traffic returning from the coast.

A well known Horsham public house which has survived to this day — The Green Dragon in the Bishopric. This must have been around the turn of the century, and the labels on the horse indicate that the occasion was possibly a carnival or some other kind of parade. The Green Dragon was one of fifty pubs in the town in the 19th century.

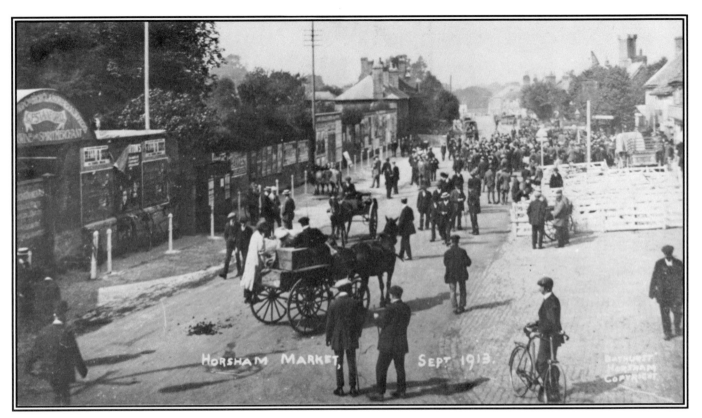

What a scene of animation the Bishopric must have presented on the weekly market day, when livestock were driven in from the neighbouring farms, and the cheapjacks and itinerent salesmen set up their stalls. This was 1913, not so very long before the market was held here for the last time, before moving to the railway station goods yard.

Another picture of the Bishopric on Market Day earlier in this century.

Narrow Middle Street in the 1930s, dominated by its One Way Traffic sign across the East end. When it was coping with two-way traffic it was not unusual for two carts to become jammed halfway. Larger folk were advised by their friends to walk sideways down this street, in case they became stuck! Tanner and Charts on the left was one of Horsham's two large drapers, the other being Chart and Lawrence.

20

Butcher's Row — or to give it the more modern name Middle Street, had a chemist's shop on the corner with the Carfax for many years. Originally it was R. Gallier, but by the time this picture was taken in the 1930s, it had become Camplins. Barclays Bank which can be seen on the right of the picture has now spread along to the corner.

East Street, c.1903 looking west towards Middle Street. A particularly vivid reminder of old Horsham, with a large number of participants. The newsagents shop on the left of the picture was that of H. J. Duffield, who published this postcard. This was before they moved to the premises formerly occupied by the Bee Hive pub, on the corner of Denne Road, in 1906.

22

East Street around 1911, viewed from the East end. The occasion was almost certainly the Coronation of King George V. One of the few shops in this street which still exists can be seen on the left, Charles Agate — corn and seed merchants.

EAST STREET, HORSHAM.

1055 Lloyd, Albury

East Street, this time from the West end looking towards the Park Street-Denne Road crossroads. Another of Horsham's splendid lamp posts is on the right. There are no vehicles, but plenty of pedestrians who were anxious to become part of history in this photograph. The period, early in this century.

24

The Scotch Wool and Hosiery Stores at No. 18 East Street, something of an institution in the 1930's. Like so many shops at this time the windows showed as wide a selection of the whole stock as possible.

EAST STREET AND RAILWAY BRIDGE, HORSHAM.

The continuation of East Street moving Eastwards, from the Park Street-Denne Road corner. In the distance can be seen the edifice always referred to as "The Iron Bridge". It is not too high, and in its time has been the cause of several mishaps with tall vehicles. This is early in the 1900's, and almost the only vehicle to be seen is a horse and cart.

Soldiers leaving Horsham in 1914, at the start of the first world war. They were being given a good send-off, although a great many were sadly never to return. The place is East Street, looking westward. The Bridge House Hotel is on the left, one of many hostelries that no longer exist.

A view of the Carfax with St. Mark's Church spire in the background. The period is around 1913, before the war memorial was built in the open space in the centre of this picture. Children are occupying their favourite meeting place on the steps of the Jubilee Fountain. Pedestrians stroll unconcernedly on the road, a horse and cart appears stationery at a most unusual angle to the roadway.

A good view of the Carfax and the Middle Street-East Street corner, looking northwards. When Middle Street was still open for traffic, this was a busy corner, controlled by a point duty policeman. Leaving the Carfax and entering East Street is a horse drawn coach, probably during the period when these vehicles were enjoying a brief come-back around 1910.

The Bandstand on the Carfax around 1895. Although the grass which once covered a large part of the Carfax has gone there was a lot more greenery at this time, than in more recent years. Local bands played regularly in the Carfax, listening to the band on a summer's evening was a popular recreation.

The Carfax was always the scene of town gatherings and celebrations. This corner in 1914 is crowded with pedestrians and vehicles, although the occasion is not apparent. One of the carts is owned by King and Barnes, the Horsham brewers, who now once again use horse drawn transport on special occasions.

A slightly more modern view of the Carfax in the late 1930's. The war memorial has been added between the Jubilee Fountain and the bandstand. At the entrance to North Street can be seen the colourful Odeon tower, which caused a good deal of local interest when it was first erected. Now it has been replaced by offices.

An unusual view of the Carfax about 1928, showing the bandstand built in 1892, and one of the buses which departed regularly from a pavement which seemed ideally suited for this purpose. The open-top deck was always popular with school boys, whatever the weather.

The bull ring and town stocks in the Carfax, 1930's. Later they were removed to the Museum, although there is now, once again a facsimile of the stocks close to this site. The last bull baiting was in 1813, the ring then remained hidden in the grass which once covered the Carfax. All the buildings in the background have now disappeared, replaced by the shopping precinct, Swan Walk.

Richardson and Sons, taxidermist and plumber, on the East side of the Carfax, in about 1880. The building later became the Horsham Building Society. Note the white coats of the workmen, shop workers were often craftsmen in those days, so it was normal to be served by someone wearing working clothes.

R. Clark, fishmonger on the inner circle (South side) of the Carfax, in the late 19th century. This was part of the premises which were later to become very well known in Horsham for Page's Perfect Pork Sausages. The wheelbarrow with Mr Clark's name on the side was evidently used for deliveries.

Lintott and Son, wholesale grocers and provision merchants at 10 The Carfax c.1890. This was a very well known local business which supplied all the many small grocer's shops in and around Horsham. Their horse-drawn carts were a familiar sight in the town and the surrounding villages. This imposing row of buildings was demolished in the late 1930s, now the site is occupied by a row of shops and flats known as "Sterling Buildings".

A newspaper report at the time headlined this, "Unusual Scene in Carfax," it took place in March 1910, when a Foden steam wagon owned by Mr W. Linfield broke through the roadway outside the Lamb Inn, one of the back wheels going into the cellar. The wagon was loaded with beer casks and had just stopped for a delivery, when the Horsham flagstone covering the cellar gave way.

Horsham's apparently ancient Town Hall, although it is only late 19th century in its present form. This nicely detailed picture dates from around the turn of the century. It shows the large sign of Cramp's Temperance Hotel on the left, run by Mr Jury Cramp, a well known, local shop owner and anti-drink campaigner. The Bear pub is on the right, but without its much loved figure of a life size bear.

Hurst Road early in this century. The building is Collyer's Grammar School, founded in Horsham in 1532. The school was moved from its Denne Road site to Hurst Road in 1893.

Horsham's Cottage Hospital in Hurst Road, opened in 1892. It ceased to be a hospital in the general sense in 1923, but is still used for out-patients. Hurst Road dates from 1870, and when this picture was taken in the early years of this century, it was still a quiet country route from the railway station to the "Common" area of the town.

THE HOSPITAL HORSHAM.

Horsham Hospital in Hurst Road, soon after its opening in the early 1920s. The gardens either side have now disappeared to make way for parked cars and a number of new wards have been built on the east side of the original building. The latest development is a completely new hospital building devoted to mental health care, which is going up behind the old hospital.

21377

Horsham. North Street.

North Street, looking towards the railway station. The time is early in this century. Two horse-drawn carts are passing on what appears to be a rather muddy street. On the right is one of Horsham's proud lamp posts which gave it the reputation of being one of the best lit towns in West Sussex.

North Street, when the railway station stood to the right of the present-day building. The date is around 1905. The large stretch of grass in the foreground is now taken-up by bus stops, phone boxes and the like. The Station Hotel in the centre of the picture, was at the time a very necessary adjunct to the rail station. Changed social habits have altered it to a popular restaurant.

Old houses in North Street, nearly opposite where the Public Library now stands. When these were removed, they were re-erected at Mannings Heath. On the left were open fields, where cattle grazed, although one was occupied by a big travelling circus in the 1930's. Now this side of North Street is given over entirely to large buildings, including Horsham Arts Centre and Park North, which houses the present Council Chamber.

HORSHAM PILGRIMS OFF TO FRANCE. AUGUST 1931.

An unusual picture from 1931 of ''Horsham Pilgrims'' off to France by train. Who the pilgrims were is not clear, although it seems likely that the expedition was connected with the Great War still only 13 years in the past. As in all photographs up to the 1930s, hats were much in evidence.

46

Another picture from the 1930's, this time the front of the older Horsham Railway Station, before it was rebuilt to the left. The band is probably the Royal British Legion, and the gentlemen lined up behind them could be more "pilgrims" as in the previous photograph.

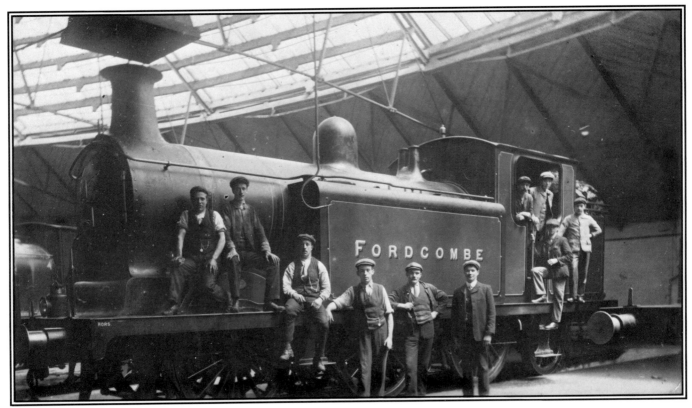

In 1905 when this photograph was taken, the locomotive shed, and indeed the goods yard itself was a very busy place. For this picture a number of the staff have assembled to proudly show their connection with one of the gentle giants they cared for.

Springfield Road during the winter of 1963. A more modern picture than most in this book, but a view which is now completely changed. A furniture shop was superimposed on the old Roman Catholic church; although the upper portion continued to betray its origins until the end. Now the buildings have been demolished, new shops will soon be occupying the site.

NORTH PARADE, HORSHAM

North Parade, as it would have appeared early in this century. Possibly one of the roads in Horsham which has changed least. The main difference is the lack of motor traffic in the picture, the nearest horse and cart seem quite happy to be on the right hand side of the road.

DOG & BACON HORSHAM

HEALEY SERIES 27

The Dog and Bacon, North Parade, early in this century. The pub is still occupying its original building, although the new premises appear to be ready for use. A little to the south of this scene there was a plank seat beloved of the "old boys", who would sit along it with their pipes, watching the comings and goings around the green.

THE DOG & BACON HOTEL, HORSHAM.
W. A. SARGOOD, Proprietor. 'Phone 25.

The Dog and Bacon again, this time in its new home, which has quickly become well covered with greenery. This is an advertising card, probably from about 1910.

52

Old Horsham Church.

The old Parish church of St. Mary, from a painting by F. Burstow in 1851. This was before the extensive restoration in 1864-5, and at this time it was essentially an English country church without the grand East window, which now adds greatly to the beauty of the building.

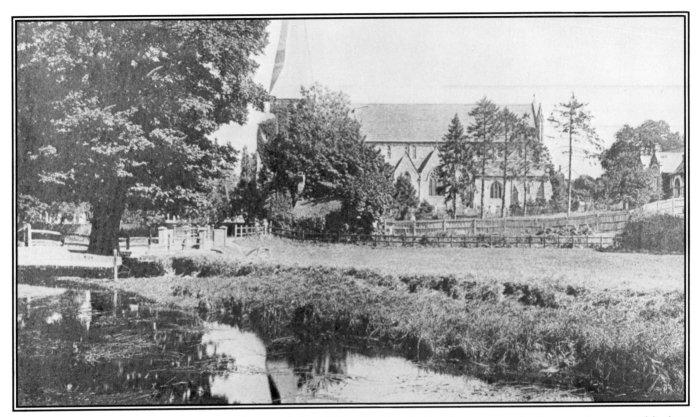

A very pleasant view of the Parish Church around the 1900's. The little bridge leads across to the area, known at this time as Mill Bay, because of its proximity to the town mill. Later this was to become a Garden of Remembrance for the Dead of the Great War.

An early 20th century view of the Parish Church, showing the seven-light East window, from the road known as Normandy. The origin of this name is not certain, it is believed to have connections with French monks, who once lived here. The Almshouses are on the left.

The Town Mill and the river around 1907. The mill dated from at least the 18th century, although the buildings changed at different periods. The area of water on the left was used for bathing by local lads, although sometimes they would arrive home less clean than when they went out.

56

Two old pictures of the Causeway in 1855. These were originally two magic lantern slides used by Thomas Honeywood, a local historian, in a series of cards of Old Horsham. The Horsham stoneslabs which feature on both the roofs and the pavements of the Causeway, may be seen on both these photographs. The right hand picture shows the scene of an alleged sighting of the ghostly figure of a cowled monk.

57

"Old Horsham"
View from Denne Hill, from the original at J. Cramp's
Fancy Shop, West Street,
Horsham.

A postcard view of Horsham, dominated by the Parish Church, from Denne Hill around the turn of the century. At this time it cost a halfpenny to post the card to anywhere in England, with certain delivery the next day — or the same day if the address was in the town. The white house on the left is believed to have been Tanbridge — the original house in Worthing Road before being rebuilt.

Horsham.

The Wrench Series, No. 8243

The Path from Denne Park.
Hill to ~~Horsham~~
Horsham

An idyllic view of Horsham from Denne Park Hill. The seat around the tree, the path and the stile were beloved of courting couples around the period of this picture, early in the 1900s. The path leads to the town via the Cricket pitch.

59

DENNE AVENUE, HORSHAM.

Entrance to Denne Park c.1906. The hill and park with its deer herd was a favourite area of quiet recreation for Horsham folk over the years. Denne Park is on the South side of Horsham, and a splendid view of the whole town may be had from the crown of the Hill. The lovely avenue of trees has now all but disappeared.

60

PICTS HILL HORSHAM HEALEY 84

Picts Hill, part of the main Worthing Road out of Horsham, as it looked around 1905. At this time heavily laden carts and early cars would have been struggling to cope with the hill as they left the town. The public house at the bottom of the hill is now called The Boar's head, but at the time of this photo it was The Fox and Hounds.

Tanbridge House, Worthing Road, formerly Horsham High School for Girls, early in this century. In 1968 it was described as "a fine example of the revived Wealden tradition, fashionable in the last two decades of the 19th century". Now it may have to make way for new houses, unless the bid to have it listed by the Department of the Environment is successful.

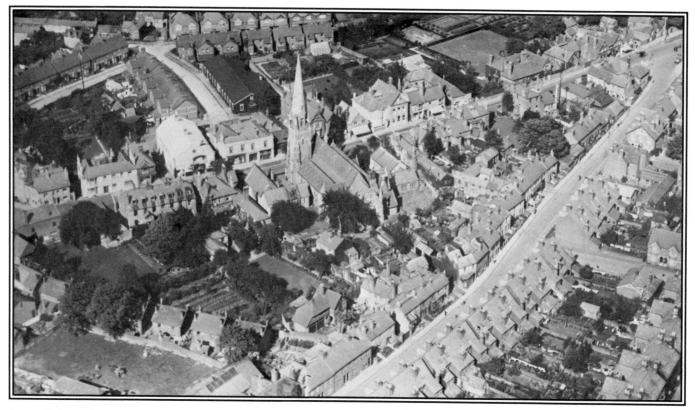

A good view of the centre of Horsham from the air, taken by Surrey Flying Services, operating from Croydon aerodrome, early in the 1920's. Park Street, North Street and part of the Carfax are clearly shown. There is also the Central Picture Hall (later The Winter Garden) in North Street, and behind it The New Hall, which had a relatively short life, later becoming the post office garage and workshop.

Fire Brigade Gala Procession at the Queen's Head Hotel, in Queen Street, 1881. Having seen other photographs of processions in a similar place, one can only conclude that this was a popular starting point. One man seems determined to get a good view, he is perched on the ironwork surrounding the Inn sign, this probably would not have impressed the landlord Mr Silvester.

Close to the Carfax at No. 6 London Road, Benjamin Blackman had his Boot Warehouse. This picture c.1909 shows the much loved old building which housed the shop, which was eventually removed despite much local criticism, to make way for new development. This part of London Road has now been re-named Medwin Walk, after a well known local solicitor, who had his offices here.

INDEN TERRACE. HORSHAM.

Little Linden Terrace enjoys its brief moment of fame in the c.1908 picture postcard. The spire of St. Mark's dominates the scene. This was the area of Horsham always known to older residents as "Back of the Post Office".

Park Street (or Back Lane as it was once known) in 1914. Evidently a parade of some kind is taking place, with a steam traction engine in the lead. Straw hats and bicycles are very much in evidence.

Denne Road around 1907. Once an important main thoroughfare, but now a leafy country lane, although only a few steps away from the centre of the town. At the time this photograph was taken, it was even quieter than today, without the occasional car to disturb its serenity.

Horsham had several mills, both water and wind. These are two windmills on Horsham Common, from a watercolour c.1858. The common occupied a large area on the north-east of the town, finally shrinking to a postage-stamp size portion of grass at the North Parade end of Trafalgar Road. The houses built in this area are all spoken of as being in "The Common" and even buses carry the name as a destination.

Mike Mill's Race in St. Leonard's Forest. The legend is that Mike, who was a smuggler ran a race with the Devil, the prize being the smuggler's soul. Afterwards no vegetation would grow along the mile-long avenue where the race took place. Another legend concerns the Lily of the Valley beds hereabouts, purported to represent St. Leonard's blood, spilt when fighting the dragon which lived in the Forest.

Opening of the Horsham Bowling Club May 17. 06

A nicely informative postcard of the opening of Horsham Bowling Club on May 17th 1906. The site was on the south side of The Bishopric. Only one player seems to have defied fashion, by appearing hatless. Photographed by a local, J. Wheeler.

Early in this century H. J. Piggott had his Oil and Colour Merchant's business at No 46 West Street. His smart van acted as an advertisement for the products he stocked. Later the business moved nearer to the Springfield Road end of the street, and subsequently across the corner to the site of Seagrave's bakers shop on the corner of the Bishopric. Photograph by W. J. Waller of 50 North Street, Horsham.

Most household and garden implements were hand-made, until mass production techniques took over. One local hand-made article which can still be bought is the besom broom. N. Rowland and Sons of Pondtail Road obviously found a ready market for their besoms in the 1920s, as this picture demonstrates.

In the early part of this century several small bus services operated in and around Horsham. One of the best known was Rayner and Son, with familiar green buses operating regular services, and for private hire. The son, Jimmie Rayner was extremely popular with passengers, having a witty remark for each stop. Here the Christ's Hospital and Barnes Green service waits on the Carfax.

Horsham Carfax looking northwards from Market Square around 1912. The decorations could be for the coronation of George V, or for one of the annual Cricket Weeks. Added interest here in the figure on the left in top hat and long frock coat, this is Horsham's Town Crier, Billy Law.

Crawley Road, Roffey, around 1905. Many of the buildings remain, the greatest difference being the lack of cars. Roffey, being a main road village, was never as attractive as some of Horsham's other neighbours. However the residents still had their pride, and it was always considered a healthier spot than Horsham, being higher than the town. The second building on the right was the Primitive Methodist Chapel.

Another picture of Crawley Road, Roffey, close to Roffey Corner. The pub The White Horse, known to all its regulars as "The Pony" is on the left. Roffey had a reputation for being a little left wing in its politics, and was sometimes spoken of as "Red Roffey".

'A Masque of Empire' given at Rudgwick. Empire Day. 1909

From 1904, Queen Victoria's birthday (May 24th) was celebrated as Empire Day, taking over from May 1st as the big day for processions and tea parties; at least as far as schools were concerned. Nowadays it is difficult to imagine how important it all was, but this picture from Rudgwick in 1909 gives some idea, as the gowned master holds forth with Brittania in the background.

Dr Frank Boxall on his rounds, crossing the ford into Surrey, near Rudgwick, in about 1900. He was the much loved village doctor, the only physician for many miles. He visited his patients by pony cart for many years, eventually giving in to the less attractive but more efficient motor car.

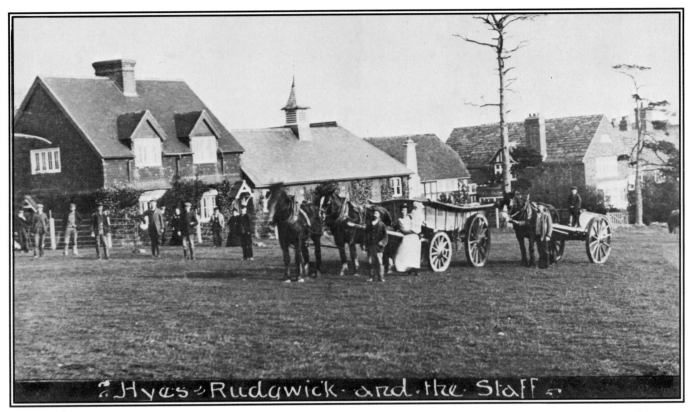

Hyes·Rudgwick·and·the·Staff

Hyes Estate Farm, Rudgwick in 1907. Although nearly in Surrey, Rudgwick always considered itself part of old Sussex. When it still had a station and regular trains, it was said that the station master would move down the train shouting "Rudgwick" opposite the First Class compartments, and changing his announcement to "Rigick" (the dialect pronunciation) when he reached the Third Class carriages.

May Day, Cowfold in 1911. The adults are admiring the children's hand made Garlands, for which the youngsters would be rewarded with pennies. May Day was also called "Garland Day". At the time of this photo the Garland ceremonies must have been starting to decline in Sussex.

The old Dun Horse public house at Mannings Heath before it was replaced by a newer building. This was probably late in the last century, when the pub had a little shop at one end. The strange vehicle outside is a cart used for transporting stags, which were released for the local stag hunt.

STATION RD. BILLINGSHURST   HEALEY 42

Billingshurst in the late 19th or early 20th century. At the time it was certainly a village, although it has now blossomed into a country town, with its own shopping precinct. The advantage of a railway station on the main London line has brought many new residents over the years.

Billingshurst High Street in 1909. The little girls seem happy to pose for the photographer, who was probably quite pleased to add this little bit of human interest to his otherwise, rather static picture.

Barnes Green Post Office in 1906. The shop was also a grocer and draper and probably carried a little of almost everything the countryman could want. The staff pose wearing their obligatory white aprons. The post office side of the business was not very profitable, but brought customers into the shop, and performed a very useful service, it was run by Mrs M. Peskett.

Another May Day Garland picture, this time from Slinfold c.1906. The children would go from door to door soliciting pennies, sometimes carrying a doll in a decorated box, which would only be disclosed on payment being received. Some people disliked children begging in this way, but most encouraged it as a charming old custom.

Haymaking on a Slinfold farm at the end of the last century. The women working alongside the men, are wearing what to us seems rather heavy clothing for a summer's day. An interesting comparison to the Land Army girls of the two World Wars.

Old House Farm, Slinfold, around the turn of the century. The carters have forsaken their smocks of an earlier age and are wearing waistcoats and jackets, and probably corduroy breeches.

Burrell Arms, West Grinstead, early in this century. The pub of this name is no more, although once it was a favourite stopping place for the local bus service. As well as some well dressed babies, the huntsmen and their hounds add interest to the picture.

Broadbridge Heath. The year is 1934 when a drought prompted Horsham Rural District Council to lay on deliveries of water twice daily. The gentleman with the bell is Mr Etheridge. Originally the water was free, later it was charged for at the rate of a halfpenny per bucket. In 1936 the village was given mains water.

"Starting on the Daily Round. The Coolham Stores". The Stores early in this century was the Post Office, and by the look of the window also carried a good line in fashionable straw hats — although the main business of the shop was grocery.

Rusper c.1908. Once described as "a village where time stood still" and certainly the present century has not succeeded in destroying it's charm. Once children were tantalised by being told about the ships in the "Rusper docks", which were about as likely as the "Faygate treacle mines". The pub on the left is the Plough.

Pease Pottage, around 1908. According to legend the name came from it being the place where prisoners on their way to Horsham Gaol were given a bowl of pottage — boiled dried peas and a piece of pork. In 1908 it must have been a very quiet place; now the M23 ends here and things tend to be a trifle busier.

The Station.   Faygate.

The railway station, Faygate, around eighty years ago. It has retained its station to the present day. One suggestion for the meaning of the name is that it was the place of the gate where fairies met, although there are less imaginative explanations.

BLUE IDOL, COOLHAM.

Coolham around 1915. The building is the strangely named Blue Idol, a Tudor farmhouse which includes the Quaker Meeting House used by William Penn and other members of The Society of Friends. The name came either from a statue of the Virgin Mary or the blue-wash used to paint the walls of the house.

Holmbush Tower near Colgate. It was built in 1855-7 by a Mr Sumner. The stone coming from the Holmbush Estate, Sumner is said to have laid every stone himself. It cost threepence to go to the top of the tower, although at one time this included a glass of lemonade. During the war the tower was used by the Home Guard, it has since been demolished.